BLACKBEARD

History Nerds

CONTENTS

INTRODUCTION

Amidst the echoes of cannon fire and the creaking timbers of warships, a legend was forged upon the churning waters of the early eighteenth century. Who could have foreseen that the Age of Sail would birth a figure so shrouded in both terror and intrigue as Blackbeard the Pirate? Sweeping across the Caribbean, vessels laden with gold spurred an era where the line between lawful privateer and lawless pirate blurred like the horizon at sea's end. Did the world create the pirate, or did the pirate remake the world? Imagine the smoke-filled chaos of a plundered merchantman, the thrill of hidden coves brimming with Spanish doubloons. Can you hear the battle cries, the thunderous volley of the Queen Anne's Revenge? And there, at the helm, stood a man whose very name would become synonymous with piracy itself. But who was the man behind the fearsome black beard? The sails billow. A storm brews on the horizon. The adventure has just begun, and the question arises: Are you brave enough to delve into the heart of the mystery? "Avast, me hearties!" The call to arms is sounded. A figure emerges from the mist, cutlass in hand, eyes alight with a fierce and burning ambition. Who was he, truly, before the legends took hold? The answer lies just beyond the reach of the turning page, where the legend of Blackbeard awaits to be unfurled...

In the waning light of a Caribbean dusk, the world seemed to hold its breath as the Age of Exploration gave way to an era of conquest and high-seas adventure. It was a time when empires expanded with the wind, when the clash of steel and the roar of cannons echoed across the ocean's expanse. Here, amidst the unruly waves of the Atlantic, history would remember the emergence of pirates as both heroes and villains, their stories woven into the fabric of maritime lore.

Travel back in time to the dawn of the eighteenth century, when the New World was a mosaic of colonies, each a jewel to be claimed by European powers. As nations vied for dominance, a side effect of their conquests sailed alongside them—piracy. Pirate havens sprouted like forbidden fruit along the trade routes, tempting sailors with the allure of freedom and fortune. The seas became a chessboard, with kings and queens plotting their moves from grand palaces, while knights in the form of privateers and pirates enacted their will upon the waves.

Historical milestones during this period were marked by the rise and fall of empires, by treaties and wars that redrew the world map. The War of Spanish Succession, for example, left in its wake a surplus of skilled seamen without ships to call home. These men, cast adrift by the tides of peace, found new purpose beneath the black flag of piracy. It was a time when the Code of the Sea dictated fairness among thieves, and honor was found among outlaws.

From past to present, the shadow of piracy looms large. Modern-day interest in these swashbuckling figures is a testament to their enduring allure, a fascination with the freedom they represent and the tales of treasure they left buried in the sands of time. The image of the pirate—bold, cunning, and undeniably charismatic—has captivated the imaginations of generations. Yet, what truths lie beneath the layers of myth and legend? How does our perception of these maritime marauders influence our understanding of history, and what lessons can we glean from their untamed lives?

Why history matters now becomes clearer when we consider the aspects of human nature that remain constant. The desire for freedom, the allure of the unknown, the dream of a life unfettered by societal constraints—these notions resonate as much today as they did during Blackbeard's time. In an age where the world seems fully charted and tamed, the pirate spirit calls to us, urging us to look beyond the horizon and question the rules that bind us.

Look to the story of one man who epitomized the pirate ideal and left an indelible mark upon the pages of history—Blackbeard. His tale is a tapestry of daring raids, fierce battles, and an unquenchable thirst for adventure. But who was the man behind the fearsome facade? What drove him to carve out a legacy that would outlast his own mortal coil?

Embark on a journey through the tempestuous life of Edward Teach, known to the world as Blackbeard. Witness the Caribbean as it once was, a world of sun-soaked islands and treacherous shoals, where the Jolly Roger flew over vessels heavy with plunder. Stand on the deck of the Queen Anne's Revenge as she cuts through the water, her sails billowing with the promise of the next conquest. Feel the tension as she draws near to her quarry, the excitement of the chase, and the rush of victory.

What led a man to embrace the path of piracy with such fervor that his name would echo through the ages? Was it rebellion, desperation, or an insatiable appetite for power? Explore the reality of pirate life, the camaraderie and the cruelty, the strategy and the spectacle. Delve into the heart of a world where every horizon hid both danger and opportunity, and every man had the chance to write his own destiny.

In these pages, you will find more than the recounting of historical events—you will discover the human experience etched within them. Through this exploration, may you come to understand the complex figure of Blackbeard, not just as a symbol of an era, but as a man who lived, breathed, and ultimately, left a legacy that would become legend.

Who was Blackbeard, truly? How did his actions shape the course of history, and why does his story continue to captivate us? The answers await as we set sail into the heart of the mystery, where the truth of Blackbeard's life is as elusive and compelling as a treasure map marked with an 'X'. The legend beckons. Will you answer the call?

THE RISE OF BLACKBEARD

Timeline of Blackbeard

Before we dissect the fascets of Blackbeards character we want to layout a timeline of events to call upon as we consider the man himself:

1680 (Approx.): Birth
Edward Teach, also known as Edward Thatch, is believed to have been born around 1680 in Bristol, England, although some records suggest he may have been born in Jamaica. His early life remains largely undocumented, but it is speculated that he came from a respectable family and received some education, which was uncommon for pirates of his time. His maritime career likely began in his youth, setting the stage for his future exploits as one of history's most notorious pirates. The lack of definitive records leaves much of his early life shrouded in mystery, contributing to his legendary status.

1701-1713: War of the Spanish Succession
During the War of the Spanish Succession, which lasted from 1701 to 1713, Teach served as a privateer for the British. Privateers were essentially legalized pirates, authorized by their governments to attack enemy ships during wartime. This period provided Teach with valuable naval experience and an understanding of maritime warfare. Privateering

served as a training ground for many pirates of the era, and it is likely where Teach honed his skills in navigation, combat, and leadership. The end of the war left many privateers unemployed, pushing them towards piracy as a means of livelihood.

1716: Joining Benjamin Hornigold

In 1716, Teach joined the pirate crew of Captain Benjamin Hornigold, a significant figure in the early stages of the Golden Age of Piracy. Hornigold operated primarily in the Caribbean and the North American east coast, and he became Teach's mentor. Under Hornigold's tutelage, Teach quickly distinguished himself and earned the captain's trust. Hornigold's decision to give Teach command of a captured sloop marked the beginning of Teach's rise in the pirate ranks. This mentorship not only provided Teach with a vessel but also with a reputation that would follow him throughout his piratical career.

Late 1716: Command of a Ship

By late 1716, Hornigold's confidence in Teach had grown, leading him to grant Teach command of a captured sloop. This significant promotion allowed Teach to begin establishing his own reputation as a pirate leader. With his own ship, Teach started conducting independent raids, targeting merchant vessels in the Caribbean. His leadership style and fearsome tactics quickly garnered respect and fear among fellow pirates and enemies alike. This period was crucial in shaping Teach's identity as Blackbeard, as he developed the fearsome persona that would make him infamous. Commanding his own ship was a pivotal step in his piratical career.

1717: Capture of the French Ship "La Concorde"
In 1717, Teach achieved a significant milestone by capturing the French slave ship "La Concorde." He renamed the vessel "Queen Anne's Revenge" and outfitted it with 40 guns, transforming it into a formidable warship. This capture marked a turning point, as the newly equipped ship enabled Teach to undertake more ambitious raids. The name "Queen Anne's Revenge" reflected Teach's possible Jacobite sympathies, hinting at political motivations behind his piracy. The acquisition of such a powerful ship significantly boosted Blackbeard's operational capabilities and his standing among pirates, cementing his status as a major threat to shipping in the Atlantic.

November 1717: Blockade of Charleston
In November 1717, Blackbeard executed one of his most audacious moves by blockading the port of Charleston, South Carolina. For nearly a week, he and his crew captured several ships attempting to enter or leave the harbor. Blackbeard's primary demand was a chest of medicine, indicating his concern for his crew's health. The blockade terrorized the local population and disrupted trade, showcasing Blackbeard's strategic acumen

and ruthless tactics. The successful blockade, coupled with his menacing appearance, enhanced his reputation as a fearsome pirate. This event exemplified Blackbeard's ability to leverage fear and power to achieve his objectives.

1717-1718: Infamy and Expansion
Between late 1717 and 1718, Blackbeard's infamy grew as he expanded his operations along the American east coast and throughout the Caribbean. His fleet captured numerous ships, amassing a significant amount of wealth and resources. Blackbeard's fearsome appearance, characterized by his long, black beard and the slow matches he lit under his hat during battle, added to his terrifying legend. His tactics were as psychological as they were physical, using his fearsome reputation to intimidate enemies into surrendering without a fight. This period marked the height of Blackbeard's power and influence in the piratical world.

June 1718: Grounding of the Queen Anne's Revenge
In June 1718, Blackbeard's flagship, the Queen Anne's Revenge, ran aground on a sandbar near Beaufort, North Carolina. The grounding of the ship was a significant setback, resulting in the loss of his most powerful vessel. Some historians speculate that the incident was intentional, possibly a ploy by Blackbeard to downsize his crew and increase his share of the loot. Following the grounding, Blackbeard and a select group of loyal followers

continued their piratical activities with a smaller, more agile fleet. Despite this loss, Blackbeard remained a formidable force, adapting to the changing circumstances.

August 1718: Pardon from Governor Eden

In August 1718, Blackbeard took advantage of a royal pardon offered by Governor Charles Eden of North Carolina. The pardon was part of a broader effort by the British Crown to suppress piracy by offering clemency to those who surrendered. Blackbeard's acceptance of the pardon was likely a strategic move, allowing him to retire from piracy without facing legal repercussions. However, he soon returned to his old ways, engaging in illicit activities and collaborating with corrupt officials. This period of semi-legitimacy highlights Blackbeard's cunning and adaptability in navigating the political landscape of the time.

November 1718: Battle of Ocracoke

On November 22, 1718, Blackbeard's life came to a violent end during the Battle of Ocracoke. Lieutenant Robert Maynard of the British Royal Navy led a surprise attack on Blackbeard's anchored ship at Ocracoke Island, North Carolina. The battle was fierce and brutal, with heavy casualties on both sides. Blackbeard fought valiantly but was ultimately killed, reportedly sustaining over twenty wounds before he fell. His death marked the end of one of the most infamous careers in pirate history.

Maynard returned to Virginia with Blackbeard's severed head as proof of the pirate's demise, cementing Blackbeard's legendary status.

1718: Posthumous Fame
Following his death in 1718, Blackbeard's legend only grew. Stories of his exploits, appearance, and ferocity were sensationalized and spread widely, creating a lasting image of the quintessential pirate. Accounts of his fearsome persona, his supposed hidden treasures, and his ruthless tactics became fodder for books, ballads, and folklore. Blackbeard's notoriety was cemented by contemporary accounts and later historical narratives, which often embellished his life story. His legacy as one of the most fearsome pirates of the Golden Age endures, influencing popular culture through numerous adaptations in literature, film, and other media.

Origins of a Pirate

The fabric of the eighteenth century was woven with threads of power, ambition, and a thirst for the unknown. As empires expanded and collided, the world bore witness to a transformation that would forever alter the course of history. It was a time of relentless exploration, of territories both claimed and contested, and of fortunes made and lost upon the high seas. It was within this crucible of change and chaos that a child was born, one whose name would become synonymous with the golden age of piracy: Edward Teach, later known as Blackbeard.

Born in the bustling port of Bristol, England, around the turn of the century, Edward's early life was framed by the cobbled streets and the towering masts that lined the docks. Bristol, a thriving hub of maritime trade, was a place where tales of the sea were as common as the salt-laden air that filled the lungs of its inhabitants. The son of a modest family, Edward was raised in a world where the horizon called louder than the church bells, where the promise of adventure was etched into the very planks of the ships that came and went with the tides.

What was it about his upbringing that set Edward on a path towards infamy? Did the stories of daring voyages and exotic lands ignite within him a flame that would one day burn as bright as the fuse of a cannon? Or was it the harsh realities of life on the docks, where survival often depended on one's ability to navigate both the treacherous waters and the equally perilous alleys of port towns?

As a youth, Edward's eyes would have watched, wide with wonder, as sailors returned from their journeys with pockets full of coin and heads full of stories. He would have learned early on that the sea was both a giver and a taker of life, its mercurial nature a reflection of the times. The lure of the ocean's call was impossible to resist. And so, like countless others before him, Edward Teach found himself drawn into the embrace of the deep blue.

What dreams did he harbor as he stood upon the bow of his first ship, the salt spray kissing his face, the wind tugging at his beard? Did he envision a life of freedom, of command, of riches beyond measure? Or were his initial aspirations more modest, simply seeking to carve out a life at sea, away from the confines of society and the predetermined role it foisted upon those born to humble beginnings?

The transition from sailor to pirate is often shrouded in mystery, a journey that takes place in the shadows of the soul as much as it does in the physical world. For Edward Teach, it was a confluence of circumstances that propelled him towards the black flag. The War of Spanish Succession had created legions of experienced seamen suddenly without purpose as peace was declared. Privateering commissions dried up, and the once clear lines between privateer and pirate blurred into oblivion.

What is it about the human spirit that revels in the idea of rebellion, that cherishes the notion of bucking the system? Perhaps it is the same sentiment that today drives us to cheer for the underdog, to root for those who dare to defy convention. Blackbeard's story taps into that primal urge to break free from the shackles of authority, to live by one's own rules. His journey from sailor to pirate was not just a career change—it was an existential pivot, a deliberate step into a life less ordinary.

Let us now delve deeper into this transformation, into the heart of a man who would come to embody the peril and promise of a pirate's life. In the pages that follow, we will trace the currents that swept Edward Teach from the docks of Bristol to the helm of the Queen Anne's Revenge. Together, we will uncover the experiences that shaped him, the choices that defined him, and the legend that would immortalize him.

Who was the man before the myth? What drove him to a life of piracy? And how did his actions leave a mark so indelible that, centuries later, we remain captivated by his story? As we peel back the layers of legend, we seek not only to understand Blackbeard the pirate but to glimpse the essence of Edward Teach, the man.

The First Noted Plunder

Amidst the tempestuous waves of the Atlantic, under the dark shroud of night that enveloped the year 1717, the brisk air carried the scent of opportunity and the whispers of destiny. Although it is unlikely that this was Blackbeard's inaugural act of piracy, it was no less a moment that would set the tone for his fearsome legacy. Records are predominately silent on when exactly he turned to villainy although it is believed to be after 1714. He is believed to have served an apprenticeship under another pirate captain called Benjamin Hornigold before becoming a pirate captain in his own right.

The moon, a silver sentinel, cast its glow upon the waters, where the shadows of ships danced with the rhythm of the sea. It was in this vast aquatic wilderness that Edward Teach, soon to be known as Blackbeard, set his eyes on his prize—a French merchant vessel laden with a bounty ripe for the taking.

The central figures in this nocturnal drama were as contrasting as the light and dark that played upon the ocean's surface. There was the French merchant ship, La Concorde, a vessel that plied the trade routes with a belly full of goods and a crew weary from their long voyage. And then there was Teach, a man whose ambition burned as fiercely as the future embers that would dance at the tip of his cannon's fuse. His crew, a motley assembly of outcasts and opportunists, mirrored their captain's hunger for a fortune that lay just beyond their grasp.

The challenge was formidable. La Concorde was no meek target; it boasted a considerable size and was guarded by a crew that would not readily surrender their cargo. Moreover, the element of surprise, so crucial to a successful assault, was threatened by the luminescent glow of the moon. Teach needed a strategy that would not only ensure victory but also cement his reputation as a force to be reckoned with on the high seas.

His approach was a blend of psychological warfare and tactical brilliance. Teach's ship, the Revenge, a sloop-of-war built for speed and maneuverability, slipped through the water like a predator stalking its prey. The dark sails, dyed to meld with the night, and the silent coordination of the crew ensured that they were upon La Concorde before an alarm could be raised. The sudden roar of cannon fire shattered the stillness, a clear message that resistance would be met with relentless fury.

The results were as swift as they were decisive. The barrage from the Revenge crippled La Concorde's masts, rendering her immobile. Teach, towering above his adversaries with a fearsome visage, led a boarding party that overwhelmed the merchant crew with a ferocity that was as calculated as it was chaotic. Within mere hours, La Concorde was his, and with it, a treasure of gold, spices, and the promise of more to come. This first plunder was not merely an act of theft; it was an announcement to the world that a new predator roamed the waters.

Yet, upon reflection, this encounter offered insights into the man behind the burgeoning myth. Teach's use of terror was not solely for the sake of cruelty but as a means to achieve his ends with minimal bloodshed. His reputation became a weapon as potent as any cannon in his arsenal, a tool that would serve him well in future confrontations.

The significance of this first plunder reached far beyond the immediate spoils. It was a microcosm of the era's shifting power dynamics, where individuals could rise from obscurity to infamy, and where the rules of engagement were written by those bold enough to wield the pen.

But what of the men who found themselves under Teach's command? What drove them to cast their lots with such a man, to embrace the perilous life of piracy? Was it desperation, adventure, or something darker that tied their fates to the black flag?

These are the questions that beckon us to delve deeper, to look beyond the surface of the tale and into the depths of the human condition. As the pages of history turn, we find that the allure of the pirate's life is as enduring as the sea itself, a siren song that calls to the rebel in all of us.

The story of Blackbeard's first plunder sets the stage for a saga of conquest and cruelty, of legend and legacy. It is a chapter in a larger narrative, one that continues to captivate and intrigue, to inspire both dread and admiration. And so, we are left to ponder: what is it about the darkness that so enchants us, that draws us into its embrace with the promise of untold treasures lurking just beneath the surface?

Rise to Infamy

In the wake of his audacious seizure of La Concorde, Edward Teach—now known far and wide as Blackbeard—was not content to rest on his laurels. His appetite for wealth and power was insatiable, and he knew that to become a legend among pirates and feared by all who sailed the seas, he would need to execute a series of grander, more daring raids. But how did he elevate himself from a mere marauder to a figure of mythical proportions? The journey was complex, fraught with peril and requiring cunning alliances. It was a path that would lead to the zenith of his infamy.

Our narrative shall guide you through the labyrinthine steps of Blackbeard's meteoric rise, and by its conclusion, you will have witnessed the transformation of a man into a legend. To tread this path, we must first consider the prerequisites for his ascent: a formidable ship, a loyal crew, an unmatched understanding of the sea, and the ability to instill fear in the hearts of his enemies.

Imagine the vastness of the ocean, the creak of timbers, the snap of sails in the wind. Blackbeard stood at the helm of his newly acquired flagship, the Queen Anne's Revenge, a vessel as formidable as its captain. Within this tale, each chapter represents a step in Blackbeard's calculated ascension—a series of raids that would not only fill his coffers but also cement his notoriety.

Let us delve into the details, where the devil, as they say, truly lies. Blackbeard's strategy was multifaceted. He targeted ships that carried the most valuable cargo—gold, jewels, weapons, and goods that could be easily traded or ransomed. His knowledge of the trade routes was unparalleled; he knew when and where to strike for maximum effect.

Have you ever wondered how one man could strike such terror into the hearts of seasoned sailors? Blackbeard's visage was a carefully crafted spectacle: his beard, as black as pitch, woven with slow-burning fuses that wreathed his head in smoke during battle, made him look like a demon conjured from the deep.

What tips can be gleaned from such a man? For those seeking to emulate his success, albeit in less felonious endeavors, the lesson is clear: reputation can be as powerful a tool as any physical weapon. But be warned, this power is a double-edged sword, one that can cut down an adversary or the wielder if not handled with care.

To validate Blackbeard's success, one need only look at the bounty he amassed and the fear he instilled. His name alone could bring a ship to surrender without a single shot fired. Yet, should you find your endeavors less successful than Blackbeard's, consider the importance of adaptability and the value of retreat as a strategic maneuver, not an admission of defeat.

Blackbeard's most infamous raid, perhaps the pinnacle of his career, was the blockade of Charleston, South Carolina. Here, he captured several ships and held the entire city ransom for a chest of medicine. It was a bold move that paid off handsomely, but it was also the beginning of his end. For with notoriety came the attention of the authorities, and with it, the inevitability of confrontation.

THE GOLDEN
AGE OF PIRACY

Piracy's Allure

In an era where the divide between the haves and the have-nots was as vast as the Atlantic itself, piracy became the siren call for the disenfranchised, the desperate, and the daring.

The seventeenth and early eighteenth centuries presented a stark reality: European powers were expanding their empires, their galleons heavy with gold from the New World, yet the common sailor lived in squalor, barely scraping by on meager wages and facing the constant threat of impressment into naval service. Herein lay the breeding ground for piracy, where the promise of wealth and autonomy lured men to cast off the shackles of servitude and seize their destinies on the high seas.

But what of the consequences if this tide of piracy went unchecked? Trade routes would be imperiled, economies could crumble, and the very fabric of empires might fray under the relentless assault of these maritime marauders. The cost of ignoring the problem was too great, the potential ruin too vast.

A solution seemed to emerge from the depths of the issue itself: offer pardons to pirates willing to lay down their arms, and integrate them into society or the official navy. By providing a path back to legitimacy, governments could quell the pirate threat while bolstering their naval forces—turning their enemies into protectors of the realm.

The steps to implement this were straightforward, albeit fraught with challenge. Proclamations of pardon needed to be dispatched to all corners of the ocean, and assurances of fair treatment had to be guaranteed. It was a delicate dance of diplomacy and force, as demonstrated when the notorious pirate Benjamin Hornigold accepted the King's Pardon and turned pirate-hunter, tracking down his former brethren for the British Crown.

Evidence of this strategy's efficacy lay in the very life of Blackbeard himself. Before his fall at Ocracoke Inlet, he too had accepted a pardon, briefly living in Bath, North Carolina, as a private citizen before returning to piracy to fund his luxurious lifestyle. This period of calm demonstrated the potential for even the most fearsome pirates to reintegrate into society.

Yet, there were those who argued for harsher measures—summary execution upon capture, no quarter given. This alternative was a crimson path, lined with the bodies of the condemned, but it risked perpetuating a cycle of violence that could swell the ranks of the pirates with each act of retribution.

The allure of piracy, with its whispered promises of riches and freedom, was a powerful force that could not be quelled by the sword alone. It required an understanding of the desperation that drove men to such a life. In the case of Blackbeard, was it not the oppressive conditions aboard merchant ships that first pushed him toward the pirate's life? Was it not the lure of equality among thieves that kept him there?

Imagine, for a moment, a world where the common sailor was treated with dignity, paid a fair wage, and given a voice. Would the call of piracy have been so irresistible? Would Blackbeard's black flag have flown so high and so long?

Through the lens of history, we see that the true solution to piracy was not merely pardons or punishment, but addressing the root of the problem—the profound inequality and injustice that prevailed at sea. Only by remedying these conditions could the world hope to extinguish the allure of piracy.

In crafting these solutions, one must remember the enduring legacy of Blackbeard. His legend serves as a stark reminder that when society fails to offer its citizens a just path, they may forge their own—no matter how perilous it may be. And so, the question that echoes through the ages is not one of how to defeat the pirates, but rather, how to heal the conditions that create them. How do we ensure that the call of the sea is not a call to arms, but a call to adventure, to discovery, to a life where one's fate is not dictated by birth, but by merit?

Only when this question is answered will the true allure of piracy be revealed: not as a path to plunder, but as a quest for the liberty and justice that every soul yearns for.

Blackbeard's Code

Beneath the fearsome façade of the pirate known as Blackbeard, there thrummed the pulse of a complex society—a society governed by codes and conventions as intricate and compelling as any nation's laws. It was within these parameters that the pirates of Blackbeard's crew navigated their treacherous world, a world in which democracy was not a mere ideal but a lived experience, albeit one marred by bloodshed and the lust for gold.

As the sun kissed the horizon, painting a crimson path across the vast Atlantic, those who sailed under the black flag found themselves not just outside the law but also creators of their own. This was not anarchy; it was a system, a pirate code established by Blackbeard himself, which dictated life aboard his vessel, the Queen Anne's Revenge.

The primary claim of this tome is that Blackbeard's pirate code was not merely a set of guidelines for thievery but a framework that established order and equity among his crew, challenging the notion that pirates were mere agents of chaos. It was a charter that straddled the line between rebellion and governance, a testament to the human desire for structure even amidst the lawlessness of the open sea.

To understand the weight of this claim, one must examine the evidence—a set of articles that

Blackbeard and his crew purportedly agreed upon. Articles such as "Every man shall have an equal vote in affairs of moment," and "Every man shall be called fairly in turn by the list on board of prizes," suggest a system where each pirate had a voice, and loot was distributed equitably. This was a stark contrast to the rigid hierarchies of naval and merchant vessels, where captains ruled with an iron fist, and the spoils were often unevenly shared.

Delving deeper into these articles reveals a society where the welfare of each member was considered. The provision for compensation for injury, with the rate set for the loss of limbs or disability, indicates an early form of insurance, a safety net for those who risked their lives in pursuit of fortune.

Yet, counterarguments abound in historical accounts that paint pirates, including Blackbeard's crew, as nothing more than cutthroats and scoundrels, with codes that were more about self-preservation than any higher principles. Some argue that the pirate code was adhered to only as long as it served the interests of the most powerful crew members, and that betrayal and violence were as common as the camaraderie and shared governance espoused in the articles.

To rebut such claims, one must acknowledge the complexity of pirate society. While it is true that treachery existed, the very existence of such a code speaks to a desire for order and justice. Moreover, historical records from trials and testimonies of pirates suggest that many truly believed in the code and saw it as essential to their survival and success.

One might further bolster this argument with tales of camaraderie and solidarity among pirates, of shared rituals, and the collective burial of treasure. These practices were not mere superstitions but reinforced the bonds that held the crew together under the flag of the code.

In conclusion, the evidence suggests that Blackbeard's pirate code was an earnest attempt at establishing a form of governance that allowed for a degree of fairness and democracy unheard of in the society from which the pirates had been ostracized. It was a radical experiment in self-governance that, though imperfect, shed light on the human capacity for creating systems of order even in the most disorderly of circumstances.

One cannot help but ponder—what drove these men to the sea, to raise the black flag against an unforgiving world? Was it mere greed or something deeper, a yearning for a sense of agency and fraternity they could find nowhere else? And what of us, the descendants of a world that birthed the likes of Blackbeard? Do we not still grapple with the same questions of governance, fairness, and the distribution of wealth?

The legacy of Blackbeard's code serves as a mirror, reflecting not just the faces of those long-gone pirates but also the visage of our present-day struggles. It is a reminder that the quest for a just society is as relentless as the tides and that, perhaps, the answers we seek lie not in the annals of the powerful but in the forgotten codes of history's outcasts.

Infamous Raids and Loots

Edward Teach was more than just a name whispered in fear among the merchant ships; he was the mastermind behind some of the most audacious raids in the Golden Age of Piracy.

In the annals of history, few have garnered such notoriety as Blackbeard. His very image—a towering man with a black beard so vast it was said he could tuck it into his belt—struck terror into the hearts of seafarers. But it was not merely his appearance that made him infamous; it was his cunning and strategy that enabled him to amass treasures beyond the wildest dreams of avarice.

Let us cast our gaze upon one raid that stands as a testament to his prowess—the siege of Charleston in 1718. The bustling port, a jewel of the American colonies, was ripe for the picking, and Blackbeard knew it. The harbor teemed with ships, each laden with wealth from the New World, and the pirate set his sights on the grand prize.

At the helm of his feared ship, Queen Anne's Revenge, Blackbeard and his crew were the main players in this daring escapade. They were outlaws, yes, but also sailors of unmatched skill, navigating treacherous waters with a confidence that belied the risks involved.

The challenge was formidable. Charleston was a fortified town, its harbor guarded by watchful eyes.

To take it by force would be folly, so Blackbeard hatched a plan that relied not on brute strength but on psychological warfare. He understood that the fear he inspired was his greatest weapon.

With his fleet, Blackbeard blockaded the port, capturing ships as they attempted to enter or leave. His approach was ruthless yet strategic, creating a stranglehold on the town's lifeline. He demanded a ransom not in gold but in medicine; a chest of apothecary supplies was his price to cease the blockade. The town, gripped by fear and unable to withstand a prolonged siege, acquiesced to his demands.

The results were staggering. Blackbeard had executed a raid without engaging in a single pitched battle, and the loot he acquired was not merely material but also strategic. The medicines were worth a fortune and essential to the well-being of his crew, a critical resource in an age when disease could decimate a ship's company faster than any battle.

Reflecting on this event, we see the dual nature of Blackbeard's leadership. On one hand, his tactics were ruthless, leveraging fear to paralyze his adversaries. On the other, they reveal a leader who valued the health and life of his men, securing for them the means to survive the perils of their profession.

While no paintings or sketches from the siege exist,

one can imagine the scene: the dark silhouette of the Queen Anne's Revenge looming over the captured merchant ships, her cannons silent but ready, the pirate flag fluttering ominously in the breeze.

This raid, among others, connects to the larger narrative of piracy as an organized challenge to the established order. It demonstrates that pirates, often dismissed as mere thieves, were capable of complex strategy and governance. They were not just rebels but also pragmatists, seeking to maximize their gains while minimizing their losses.

Now, consider this: in our condemnation of piracy, do we not overlook the ingenuity and resourcefulness that these outlaws exhibited? Is there not a form of audacious brilliance in the way Blackbeard and his kind turned the tables on the so-called civilized world?

Blackbeard's legacy is a mosaic of terror and fascination, a man larger than life, commanding the sea with a mix of brute force and shrewd calculation. As history records the infamy of his name, it also can't help but acknowledge his place as one of the most formidable figures to have ever hoisted the black flag.

In pondering the echoes of Blackbeard's exploits, we are compelled to ask ourselves: What drives a man to reject the shackles of society and seek fortune on the high seas? Is the outlaw merely a criminal, or is there something more—a rebel heart beating to the rhythm of freedom and adventure?

The story of Blackbeard is not just one of raids and loots; it is a narrative that challenges us to look beyond the surface, to understand the complexities of human nature and the lengths to which one will go to carve a name in the annals of eternity.

THE LEGEND OF BLACKBEARD

Tales From the Seven Seas

In the annals of maritime lore, few figures capture the imagination quite like the infamous pirate Blackbeard. His very name conjures images of billowing sails on the horizon, the creak of timbers, and the flutter of the black flag. We've learned about the rise of Blackbeard, but who was the man behind the legend, and where does the truth lie within the web of myths spun around him?

As history's quill first dipped into the inkwell of Blackbeard's tale, it painted a portrait of a man shrouded in mystery. Edward Teach—or Thatch, as some records claim—rose like a specter from the misty waters of the early 18th century. From here, let us embark on a voyage through time, navigating the choppy waters of history to uncover the origins of this most notorious pirate.

The curtain rises on our tale in the sugarcane-laden islands of the Caribbean, where Blackbeard first hoisted his flag as a privateer during Queen Anne's War. His transition from privateer to pirate marked the first significant crest in the wave of his legend and although the date is not exact it is believed to have been after 1714. The seas he roamed were treacherous, not just for their swirling currents, but for the men who sailed them—men who often blurred the lines between lawful combatants and outlaws. Blackbeard's fearsome reputation grew with each plundered vessel, each tale of terror whispered in the taverns of port towns.

Visual aids are not mere embellishments; they serve as a lantern in the murky depths of history. Picture, if you will, a map dotted with X's marking the conquests of Blackbeard's ship, the Queen Anne's Revenge. Imagine the line tracing his path from the Caribbean to the American colonies, where his legend would reach its zenith.

As we chart the course of Blackbeard's saga, we cannot ignore the diversity of its tellers. In England, his story was a cautionary tale of criminality; in the Americas, an emblem of untamed freedom. Cultural variations colored the canvas of his life, adding layers of complexity to the man beneath the black hat.

What then, are we to make of the modern Blackbeard? His image has been resurrected in novels, films, and even children's cartoons. Each interpretation dons a new coat of varnish on the hull of his legacy. In these tales, he is as often a charming rogue as he is a fearsome brigand, a testament to our fascination with the duality of his character.

Yet, not all voyages are smooth sailing. Blackbeard's story is awash with controversies, from disputes over his final resting place to the veracity of his supposed buried treasure. The most notable turning point in his narrative was the fateful encounter with Lieutenant Maynard in the waters off Ocracoke

Island. The battle that ensued saw the end of Blackbeard, his head severed and displayed as a grim trophy—his final passage from man to myth.

How does one then distill truth from legend in the tale of Blackbeard? Can we ever hope to separate the man from the myth? Perhaps the answer lies not in the details we can prove but in the stories we choose to tell. For in these stories, Blackbeard sails on, as much a creation of our collective imagination as the flesh-and-blood pirate who once stalked the Seven Seas.

So, dear reader, I pose to you a direct question: Is it not the mark of a truly enduring legend to exist beyond the confines of fact, to become a narrative etched indelibly into the fabric of culture? Aye, Blackbeard's flag may have been struck from its mast, but his tale remains aloft in the winds of history, unfurled and unyielding.

In the world of pirates, Blackbeard reigns supreme. His name alone can still send a shiver down the spine of even the saltiest sea dog. But what of Edward Teach, the man behind the beard? His story is not one of simplicity, but a complex tale woven from threads of fact and fiction, and it is this very complexity that beckons us ever deeper into the fathomless depths of his legend.

Show, don't tell, they say. Thus, I leave you with the image of Blackbeard's silhouette against a blood-red sunset, his figure merging with the darkness as day gives way to the black of night—a fitting metaphor for a man who has become one with the shadows of myth.

Fear and Fascination

In the theater of the high seas, where the drama of life and death was played out beneath the unfurling sails of the Age of Piracy, no actor commanded the stage quite like Blackbeard. He was a master of psychological warfare, his very presence on the ocean a calculated performance designed to strike terror into the hearts of his adversaries. At the same time, Blackbeard's persona elicited a contradictory allure, a magnetism that drew the masses into a spell of morbid curiosity and admiration. It's within this juxtaposition of fear and fascination that we delve into the heart of Blackbeard's legacy.

The purpose of our exploration is to dissect the intricate strategies Blackbeard employed to cultivate his menacing reputation and the public's simultaneous dread and intrigue. To do this, we must first establish criteria: the methods of instilling fear and the elements that fuel fascination.

Let us then direct our spyglass to the past. Blackbeard's ship, the Queen Anne's Revenge, was an imposing sight, her cannons like the teeth of a leviathan ready to devour any who dared approach. Accounts of Blackbeard's appearance—his towering frame, the smoldering fuses woven into his beard— served to amplify his formidable image. These tales also bore a striking resemblance to the theatricality of stage villains, men who wore their malice like a cloak, draped over broad shoulders for all to see. In this way, Blackbeard shared the stage with such characters, his likeness to them undeniable.

Yet, contrast this with Blackbeard's unexpected displays of mercy; his captives were often released unharmed, their vessels spared from destruction. This divergence from the merciless pirate archetype added complexity to his character. Was he the merciless demon as some accounts suggested, or a calculating tactician, aware that fear could be wielded more effectively than the sword?

Visual aids are absent here, but one can imagine the juxtaposition of Blackbeard's imposing figure against the backdrop of his unexpected leniency as a powerful image, a duality captured in a single frame.

The analysis of these parallels and contrasts reveals a man who understood the power of reputation. Blackbeard cultivated his image, knowing that the more fearsome he appeared, the less likely he would have to engage in actual combat—a tactic that preserved his men and resources. Still, the fascination with his persona suggests that people are drawn to that which they fear, a paradox that lies at the heart of the human condition.

What are the broader implications of this dynamic? Blackbeard's recognition of the psychological impact of fear indicates an early understanding of what modern psychology would describe as the intimidation factor. It also speaks to the timeless allure of the antihero, a figure who defies societal norms and commands attention through a blend of dread and awe.

In terms of real-world relevance, one can draw parallels between Blackbeard's psychological tactics and modern branding strategies. Entities, from corporations to celebrities, craft images that elicit specific emotional responses, curating a blend of awe and approachability akin to the duality of Blackbeard's persona.

So, what can one conclude from this juxtaposition of fear and fascination? It seems Blackbeard's legend is not just a relic of the past but a case study in the enduring power of narrative and perception. He was a man who knew the value of image and used it to his advantage, leaving a legacy that transcends time.

As the sun dips below the horizon, casting the sea into twilight, one might wonder at the enduring allure of the pirate known as Blackbeard. Can we truly separate the man from the myth, or is it the interplay between the two that captures our imagination? With every retelling, the line between Edward Teach and Blackbeard blurs until they become inseparable—a single entity occupying a space where history and legend coalesce.

Indeed, the name Blackbeard continues to echo through the ages, a haunting reminder of the power of infamy and its strange bedfellow, allure. In this dance of darkness and light, one thing remains clear: Blackbeard's shadow looms large, a figure etched not just in the annals of maritime history but in the very psyche of humankind.

The Icon of Piracy

In the collective consciousness of society, Blackbeard's image looms as large as the fearsome sails of his ship once did on the horizon. His legacy, an intricate web of myth and reality, has been spun across the centuries, finding its way into every medium of popular culture. From swashbuckling tales to silver screen epics, Blackbeard has become the iconic emblem of piracy. But what does this transformation from man to legend reveal about our society and its fascination with outlaws and rebels?

To delve into this phenomenon, one must first recognize the human penchant for storytelling and its power to shape perspectives. The saga of Blackbeard has been told and retold, each iteration adding layers to his mythos. Literary works, such as Robert Louis Stevenson's "Treasure Island," paved the way for Blackbeard's image as the quintessential pirate, despite the fact that the character Blackbeard himself doesn't appear in Stevenson's narrative. It is the essence of the man, the aura of danger and adventure, that has been distilled into our cultural understanding of piracy.

Venture into the realm of cinema, and you'll find Blackbeard portrayed with a certain romanticism, despite his historical reputation as a ruthless marauder. Films like "Pirates of the Caribbean" and "Blackbeard, the Pirate" have contributed to a certain heroic framing of pirates, presenting them as charming rogues rather than the brutal outlaws of maritime history. These portrayals often overlook the harsh realities of piracy, choosing instead to focus on the freedom and rebellion that piracy symbolizes. Why does society gravitate towards such romanticized depictions, you might ask?

Consider the allure of the open sea, the unshackling from society's constraints—it's a narrative that resonates deeply with our innate desire for freedom and autonomy. Blackbeard, in his lawlessness and mastery of his fate, embodies the spirit of independence that many yearn for. Yet, this admiration is not without its contradictions.

For every tale that glorifies the pirate life, there is an undercurrent of truth that speaks to the violence and brutality of the era. Blackbeard's own end—killed in a fierce battle with the Royal Navy—serves as a stark reminder of the peril that accompanied the life of a pirate. This dichotomy between the romanticized fantasy and the grim reality creates a tension that is both intriguing and unsettling. Is it the danger that captivates us, or the escape it represents from the mundane safety of our everyday lives?

Turning to the facts, records from the 18th century provide evidence of Blackbeard's reign of terror on the seas. Yet, these same historical documents also reveal instances of mercy and cunning that contradict the image of a mindless brute. Blackbeard was known to rely on his fearsome reputation to avoid bloodshed, a tactic that speaks to a shrewdness not often associated with piracy. It is this complexity that makes his story so enduringly fascinating.

To truly grasp the nuances of Blackbeard's portrayal, one must also understand the language of piracy. Terms like "scallywag" and "buccaneer" have found their way into our lexicon, often stripped of their original menacing connotations. This sanitization of pirate terminology reflects a broader tendency to romanticize the past, to view it through a lens that softens its harsher realities.

As we conclude this exploration of Blackbeard's iconic status, it is clear that his legacy is more than just a testament to the power of narrative; it is a mirror reflecting society's complex relationship with its outlaws and antiheroes. In Blackbeard, we find a character who defies the order, who commands both fear and admiration, and whose story has been shaped as much by the tales spun about him as by the truths they obscure.

So, what are the key takeaways from this examination of Blackbeard's enduring image? It seems that our society is drawn to the dichotomy embodied by this legendary pirate— the clash between freedom and anarchy, between the romanticized ideal and the historical reality. Blackbeard's transformation into the icon of piracy tells us that we are captivated by the rebel, enthralled by the notion of living outside the rules, yet we are also comforted by the distance time provides from the true brutality of his world.

In the end, Blackbeard's legacy is not just about the man, nor is it solely about the legend; it is about the ongoing conversation between the two, a dialogue that reveals our deepest fears and aspirations. As we chart the waters of our own lives, we find in Blackbeard's story a strange kinship, a reminder that within the heart of society, there always beats a longing for the adventure and allure of the untamed sea.

THE DOWNFALL
OF BLACKBEARD

The King's Pardon

In an age when the crash of cannon fire and the harsh cry of seagulls were as common as the creak of wood beneath one's feet, a dilemma of loyalty and survival whispered through the salt-laden winds of the Caribbean. It was an era where the distinction between villain and hero was as blurred as the horizon line melding sea to sky.

Pirates, the scourge of the seven seas, had become a force so formidable that even the mightiest of empires found themselves at a loss. Among these buccaneers, one name rose to infamy above all others: Blackbeard. But it was not his fearsome appearance nor his legendary exploits alone that captivated the collective consciousness; rather, it was his dance with the devil of legitimacy— the King's Pardon—that posed a question echoing through the annals of history: What drives a man to forsake the gallows' shadow for the false promise of redemption, only to return to his darkened path once more?

It was 1718 when the Crown, desperate to cleanse the waters of the pirate menace, extended an olive branch dipped in the ink of politics and power. This Royal Pardon, a decree of absolution, was the Crown's gambit to quell the pirate threat—a chance for these outlaws to wipe their slates clean in the eyes of the law.

As the proclamation made its way from one pirate haunt to the next, the impact was immediate and profound. Men who had spent their lives in the thrall of freedom's siren song now faced a choice that cut to the very marrow of their existence: Continue in their ways and risk the noose or accept the King's mercy and live a life within the confines of the law.

Blackbeard's acceptance of the pardon was a turn of events that sent ripples across the Caribbean. The fearsome pirate, who had stood as a symbol of defiance against the world's greatest navies, now seemingly bowed before the throne. Yet the calm that followed was as deceiving as the stillness before the storm.

To understand the depth of this decision, one must first grasp the life that Edward Teach, known to many as Blackbeard, had led. He was a man who, like many of his kind, had found in piracy not just a means to survive but a way to thrive beyond the reach of kings and courts. His black flag, emblazoned with the image of a skeleton spearing a heart, was a stark reminder of the price of crossing him.

The personalization of Blackbeard's tale lies in a little-known encounter on the shores of what is now North Carolina. Here, amidst the whispering sands and the watchful eyes of his crew, Blackbeard confided in a young sailor, a lad no older than sixteen, who had been pressed into piracy by the dire straits of his own life. "The sea, she is both mother and executioner," Blackbeard had said, "On her bosom, we find life and just as swiftly, she can take it away." This intimacy of choice, the crossroads of destiny, was a moment that encapsulated the essence of the pirate's plight.

The stakes were undeniably high. Acceptance of the pardon meant more than simply abandoning a life of piracy; it was a relinquishment of identity, a submission to the very powers that many had taken to the sea to escape. For Blackbeard, it was a gamble—a play that hinted at a strategy beyond the comprehension of the Crown.

The path ahead, though shrouded in the mists of time, offers us insights into the human heart. Blackbeard's eventual return to piracy, despite the risks, suggests a complexity of character and motivation that is the heart of our exploration. In the rest of this chapter, the layers of this enigma will be peeled back, revealing the man behind the myth.

Why, then, did Blackbeard accept the pardon only to discard it like a snake shedding its skin? Was it a momentary lapse in judgment, a failure of nerve, or perhaps, a deeper ruse designed to serve a purpose only he could fathom?

The answer to this question is not one we will find etched in the ledgers of history, nor whispered in the tales of old. It is an answer that lies buried in the psyche of a man who defied an empire, who sought freedom in an unfree world, and who, when presented with the chance to step away from the legend he had become, chose instead to burn brighter, if only for a moment, before the darkness claimed him.

As we delve deeper into the story of Blackbeard and the King's Pardon, we will explore the intricate dance of a man on the edge of two worlds, ever teetering between the pull of the gallows and the call of the wild sea. It is a tale that will challenge us to question our own convictions and the lengths to which we would go to hold fast to what we hold dear. It is a journey, dear reader, that we will take together, as we seek to uncover the truth behind the notorious pirate's fateful choices.

So, I ask you: What is the price of a man's soul on the open market of morality? And what currency is sufficient to purchase the freedom of the unfettered heart? These are the questions that lie at the heart of our story, the answers to which we will seek in the pages to come.

The Final Battles

As dawn broke over the Ocracoke Inlet on the 22nd of November, 1718, a chill hung in the air, foretelling a confrontation that would etch itself into the annals of maritime lore. The stage was set for the final act in the life of the pirate known as Blackbeard. The waters, which had once cradled him in their embrace, were poised to become his battleground—and his grave.

For any who dared to navigate the treacherous journey that was Blackbeard's downfall, certain elements were indispensable. A keen understanding of naval tactics, an intimate knowledge of the labyrinthine waterways of the Carolina coast, and a crew of unwavering loyalty were but a few of the prerequisites. The impending battle was not just a clash of ships and swords, but of wits and wills.

To the untrained eye, the plan seemed simple: Lieutenant Robert Maynard of the Royal Navy had been dispatched with two sloops, the Ranger and the Jane, to capture or kill the notorious pirate. Yet, the operation was fraught with complexity. The sloops were chosen for their shallow drafts, capable of navigating the shallow Pamlico Sound, and their crews were handpicked for their tenacity.

The strategy unfurled in stages. Maynard's orders were to find and engage Blackbeard, whose sloop, the Adventure, lay in wait. Intelligence suggested that Blackbeard, having recently returned to piracy, had let his guard down, celebrating with his crew and taking on supplies. Maynard would use this to his advantage.

As the Royal Navy vessels approached, Blackbeard's lookout spotted them. But Maynard, with cunning foresight, had hidden most of his men below decks, creating the illusion of being undermanned. The deception worked. Confident in his numerical superiority, Blackbeard commanded his crew to ready the cannons and prepare to board.

The battle commenced with the roar of cannon fire, the acrid smoke of gunpowder blurring the lines between sea and sky. Blackbeard's initial salvo tore into the Jane, wounding Maynard's cause but not his resolve. The Lieutenant ordered the return fire, and the ballet of bombardment continued, each side trading blows in a deadly cadence.

In the midst of this chaos, Maynard's strategy unfolded. As the Adventure maneuvered for another pass, Maynard's sloops closed in. Aboard the Ranger and the Jane, the hidden men emerged, revealing the true strength of the opposition. Blackbeard, caught off guard but not defeated, rallied his men for a brutal melee.

The clash of steel rang out as the pirates and the navy men met in combat. Blackbeard, a towering figure with slow-match fuses smoking in his beard, fought with the ferocity of a cornered beast.

Maynard and Blackbeard faced off in a duel that would become legendary. The pirate's cutlass met the lieutenant's sword in a flurry of sparks and shouts.

Remember, those who engage in battles of such magnitude must be prepared to adapt. The shifting tides, the unpredictable winds, and the courage of your adversary are all variables that can turn the tide in an instant.

To verify the success of such a confrontation, one need only look to the outcome. Blackbeard, though a formidable opponent, ultimately fell. Maynard's sword, aided by the blades of his men, found its mark repeatedly until the pirate legend lay defeated, his lifeblood mingling with the saltwater that had been his home.

For those seeking to understand the victory, it was not merely in the death of a pirate but in the dismantling of a myth. The Royal Navy's triumph over Blackbeard signaled the beginning of the end for the Golden Age of Piracy. It was a validation of strategy, courage, and the unwavering execution of duty.

However, even the best-laid plans can encounter unforeseen challenges. Should one find themselves in a similar situation, facing an enemy as cunning as Blackbeard, it is crucial to remain vigilant, to anticipate the unexpected, and to adapt swiftly to the ever-changing dynamics of battle.

In the aftermath, Lieutenant Maynard displayed Blackbeard's severed head upon the bowsprit of his ship—a grim trophy and a stark warning to any who would follow in the pirate's footsteps. The final battles of Blackbeard had come to an end, the smoke cleared, and the sea calmed once more, but the legend of the fearsome pirate would live on, whispered in the wind and woven into the fabric of maritime history.

In the flesh, Blackbeard was mortal, but in death, he became something more—a symbol of the untamable spirit of the sea. And so we must ask ourselves: What is the legacy of a man who defied empires and lived and died by the sword? How do we weigh the terror he wrought against the dark allure of his freedom?

These are questions not easily answered, for they delve into the very depths of human nature. The story of Blackbeard is a canvas painted with the broad strokes of adventure and the fine lines of morality. It is a tale of a man who became a legend, and a reminder that even the mightiest among us are but whispers on the ocean breeze.

Legacy in Tatters

In the wake of Blackbeard's demise, the waters of the Atlantic seemed to quiet, as if in respect for the fallen marauder. The world had borne witness to the curtain fall on an era of high-seas villainy, with the death of Edward Teach, better known as Blackbeard, at its briny heart. The blood-tinted waves around Ocracoke Inlet whispered tales of the fierce encounter, carrying them to distant shores and into the annals of history.

With the scent of gunpowder still lingering over the inlet, the remnants of Blackbeard's crew found themselves adrift in a world that suddenly seemed much larger and more unforgiving. For these men, the loss of their captain was more than the demise of a fearsome leader; it was the collapse of an ideology. Blackbeard had been their compass in the lawless expanse of the ocean, and without him, their future was a map with no destination.

These outlaws, once united under the black flag of their captain's ambition, now faced a reckoning. Some attempted to vanish into the coastal settlements, their identities obscured by the very obscurity of their existence. Others clung to the fraying edges of their fraternity, seeking to rekindle the flame that Blackbeard had lit in their hearts. But the tide had turned, and the Golden Age of Piracy was waning, its luster dimming with each passing day.

The impact of Blackbeard's death rippled across the Atlantic, reaching as far as the cobblestone streets of London and the hallowed halls of the Admiralty. The triumph over the pirate and his crew was lauded as a decisive blow against the scourge that had plagued the seas. Merchants breathed easier, and navies stood taller, basking in the glow of a hard-won victory. Yet, beneath the veneer of celebration, there was an unspoken understanding that the sea was an indomitable force, and its siren song would always give rise to men like Blackbeard.

Do the ghosts of men such as Blackbeard truly rest, or do they roam the waves, seeking vessels to command in the night's darkest hours? The question is as enigmatic as the man himself, for his end was not the conclusion of a story but the beginning of a legend.

How does one measure the legacy of a pirate? Is it in the gold he plundered, the fear he inspired, or the stories that survived him? Blackbeard's name became synonymous with the terror of the unknown, a reminder that beyond the reach of the law lay men who bowed to no crown, no creed, but their own.

Yet, history is a mirror reflecting the countless facets of truth. Blackbeard's legacy is not solely one of bloodshed and terror; it is also a tale of freedom, of rebellion against the constraints of a society that many felt had failed them. It speaks to the allure of the horizon and the human yearning to escape the chains of convention.

In this present age, where the spirit of piracy is romanticized in tales for children and blockbuster films, one must ponder the true nature of Blackbeard's end. Has the world learned from the chaos he wrought, or does it cling to the myth, enamored with the fantasy of unfettered liberty on the high seas?

The legacy of Blackbeard, much like the wreckage of his final battle, lies scattered across the ocean floor of our collective consciousness. It is a puzzle that challenges us to piece together the fragments of a life lived in the shadows of infamy and to discern the man behind the myth.

Let us then set sail from the historical shores of Blackbeard's time, navigating toward the modern understanding of his impact. We embark on a voyage that explores not only the deeds of the man but the imprint he left upon the world. It is a journey through the murky waters of morality, where hero and villain often share the same deck.

For as long as ships brave the vast embrace of the sea, the name Blackbeard will echo in the creak of timbers and the snap of sails. His story, a tapestry of fear, fascination, and freedom, continues to captivate those who hear it. What, then, is the essence of his enduring allure? Could it be that within his tale lies a dark reflection of our own desires—to break the chains, to live by our own code, to be remembered long after the final breath escapes us?

The legacy of Blackbeard, though tattered by time and tarnished by legend, remains an indelible part of our past. It is a legacy that challenges us to look beyond the surface, to seek the man beneath the black hat, and to understand that history is not merely a collection of dates and events, but a mosaic of human lives, each with a story that deserves to be told.

UNEARTHING
BLACKBEARD

The Hunt for the Queen Anne's Revenge

In the murky depths off the coast of North Carolina, where the confluence of the Gulf Stream and Labrador Current creates a swirling dance of the Atlantic, a vestige of the past lay hidden for centuries. Here, in the waters near Beaufort Inlet, an intrepid group of marine archaeologists would uncover the skeletal remains of what was once the most feared vessel to navigate these seas—the Queen Anne's Revenge, the flagship of the notorious pirate Blackbeard.

The main players in this underwater odyssey were a dedicated team from the North Carolina Department of Natural and Cultural Resources, supplemented by a cadre of volunteers, historians, and conservation experts. Among them was Dr. Sarah Jennings, whose expertise in colonial maritime history made her an anchor in the endeavor. Her counterpart, the seasoned underwater archaeologist James McKeon, brought with him a wealth of experience in shipwreck discovery and excavation.

The challenge they faced was formidable: locate and excavate a ship that had not been seen since it ran aground in 1718. The Queen Anne's Revenge was more than a ship; it was a legend, a specter from an age when pirates ruled these waters with impunity.

The team's mission was not only to find the ship but to piece together a tangible narrative of life at sea during the Golden Age of Piracy.

Their approach combined meticulous research with advanced technology. Historical records, including maps and eyewitness accounts, were scoured for clues, while sonar, magnetometers, and remotely operated vehicles (ROVs) played pivotal roles in the search. Once the site was located, painstaking excavation efforts began, with divers carefully documenting and recovering artifacts from the ocean floor.

The results were nothing short of extraordinary. Cannons, anchors, gold dust, medical instruments, and personal items emerged from the sediment, each with a story to tell. The most significant find was a large bell inscribed with the year 1705, providing a silent testament to the ship's identity. Over 30 cannons were identified, indicating the formidable nature of Blackbeard's flagship.

Analysis of the artifacts painted a vivid picture of life aboard the Queen Anne's Revenge. The weaponry suggested a ship prepared for battle, while medical supplies indicated a concern for crew welfare. Personal items, like clothing fragments and smoking pipes, hinted at the daily life and diversity of the crew.

Visual aids were crucial in bringing the story to life for the public. Detailed diagrams of the ship's layout, photographs of the artifacts, and even 3D reconstructions allowed people to visualize the vessel and its contents, bridging a gap of over three hundred years.

The story of the Queen Anne's Revenge was more than just a tale of piracy; it was a window into a period of significant historical upheaval. The ship's presence in American waters spoke to the complex relationships between Europe, Africa, and the Americas during the early 18th century. It exemplified the entangled nature of trade, colonialism, and piracy, and the push-pull of lawlessness and governance on the high seas.

As the final artifacts were conserved and the last reports were filed, a question lingered in the salty air: What other secrets did the Queen Anne's Revenge still conceal? The excavation had provided answers but also opened new avenues of inquiry, inviting scholars and enthusiasts alike to delve deeper into the maritime mysteries of Blackbeard's time.

The story of the Queen Anne's Revenge was far from over; it had merely surfaced for a breath before diving back into the depths of history, where it would continue to captivate the imaginations of those who dared to chase its wake. What new revelations would the future hold, and what further insights might be gleaned from the deep? Only time, and the relentless pursuit of knowledge, would tell.

Forensic Revelations

In the shadow of the Queen Anne's Revenge's mystique, a new chapter of Blackbeard's legacy has been prised open by the meticulous hands of forensic science. The treasures and trinkets, once interred with the infamous ship, now yield clues far more valuable than gold: they offer us an unprecedented glimpse into the life and health of one of history's most enigmatic figures—Edward Teach, known to many as Blackbeard.

Delving into the heart of this forensic exploration, one finds a narrative punctuated by bone fragments and isotopic signatures, each piece contributing to a story pieced together like a puzzle by the diligence of modern science. The claim that arises from this endeavor is bold yet supported by the concrete: these remains and artifacts provide new insights into the health, origins, and very humanity of the pirate once thought to be more myth than man.

Primary evidence to bolster this claim comes from the analysis of skeletal remains believed to be associated with the crew of the Queen Anne's Revenge. Found in close proximity to the shipwreck, these bones whisper tales of scurvy and malnutrition, conditions common among seafarers of the 18th century. The teeth, specifically, speak volumes, with their signatures of lead and mercury, likely from medical treatments of the time, painting a vivid picture of the ailments and the rudimentary cures that plagued Blackbeard's crew.

As we delve deeper, the chemical composition of the bones offers more than just a glimpse into the health conditions—they hint at origins and travels. Strontium isotope analysis, for instance, suggests diverse geographical backgrounds for the crew, aligning with historical accounts of Blackbeard's melting pot of pirates from different corners of the world. These isotopic signatures ground the legend in reality, suggesting a life on the seas that was both arduous and cosmopolitan.

However, there are counter-evidence and counterarguments that challenge these findings. Skeptics argue that the remains may not be directly linked to Blackbeard or his crew. After all, the waters where the Queen Anne's Revenge found her final resting place were trafficked by numerous sailors over centuries. Could these bones belong to later victims of the sea's caprices?

In rebuttal, forensic anthropologists turn to the artifacts found alongside the remains—buttons, buckles, and weaponry—that can be dated back to the early 18th century, aligning with the time of Blackbeard's last stand. Moreover, the location of the remains, within the shipwreck's debris field, strengthens the argument that they likely belonged to the Queen Anne's Revenge's ill-fated crew.

Further evidence comes from the analysis of lead shot and gun flints, which through elemental analysis, have been traced to English origins, again consistent with Blackbeard's known armaments and his predilection for British weaponry. These small details contribute to the larger narrative, corroborating the origins and practices of the crew that once sailed under the black flag.

As we approach the conclusion of this forensic odyssey, we return to the heart of our initial assertion. The evidence, in its multitude of forms —from bone chemistry to metallurgic signatures— reinforces the claim that the remains and artifacts from the Queen Anne's Revenge provide fresh insights into Blackbeard's life and the health of his crew. These findings, once submerged beneath the ocean's waves, now emerge to rewrite the narrative of one of the sea's most notorious figures.

In the end, as the sun sets on the horizon of this forensic journey, we are left to ponder the humanity of those who once stood on the shifting decks of the Queen Anne's Revenge. What tales could they tell if their lips could speak beyond the grave? And what new revelations will the relentless pursuit of knowledge unveil about the enigmatic Blackbeard and his motley crew? With each uncovered artifact and analyzed bone, the legend continues to unfold, revealing a tapestry of history woven with threads of fact and fiction, waiting for the next curious mind to explore its depths.

The Pirate's Enduring Mystique

Blackbeard's tale, a tapestry of intrigue and terror on the high seas, has endured through centuries, captivating the imagination like few other figures in history. But what is it about this particular pirate that continues to hold our collective gaze, refusing to be relegated to the dusty annals of time? The answer lies not just in the deeds of the man, but in the ongoing narrative shaped by archeology and scholarship.

To comprehend fully the fascination with Edward Teach, better known as Blackbeard, one must venture beyond the surface of swashbuckling legend. The pirate's life was a complex one, interwoven with the social and political fabric of the 18th-century Caribbean. He was a man of his time, embodying the fears and fascinations of an era when the New World was ripe with both opportunity and danger.

Imagine the scenes that played out aboard the Queen Anne's Revenge: the roar of cannons, the smell of gunpowder, and the sight of the Jolly Roger snapping in the ocean wind. These vivid imageries are not just the creations of novelists; they are derived from historical accounts, from the testimonies of those who witnessed Blackbeard's reign on the Atlantic.

But let us take a moment to consider the research that breathes life into history. Archeological excavations of shipwrecks attributed to Blackbeard, like the Queen Anne's Revenge, unearth not just artifacts but stories. When archeologists discovered a cache of medical instruments aboard the wreck, it wasn't just the metal and glass that were cataloged —it was the silent testament to the care, however rudimentary, taken to keep a crew of outlaws alive and well enough to plunder.

How do we reconcile the image of a terror of the seas with that of a captain who saw to his crew's medical needs? This is where scholarship plays a crucial role, knitting together the fragments of evidence into a coherent narrative. Scholars pore over privateer contracts, logbooks, and even the trial records of Blackbeard's crew to understand the economic and legal nuances of piracy.

The data and facts brought to light by these efforts paint a picture of a man who was not just a pirate but also a shrewd leader who operated within the complex mercantile systems of his day. Blackbeard strategically used the threat of violence more often than violence itself, a tactic that ensured his notoriety while often sparing his crew from bloody confrontation.

What must it have been like to stand on the deck of a ship, the salt air mixing with the tension of an impending boarding? The thrill and dread, the camaraderie and betrayal—all these elements are embedded in the accounts and records that have survived time's relentless passage.

To the layperson, terms like "isotopic analysis" or "forensic anthropology" might seem impenetrable, but they are keys that unlock the past. By clarifying these terms, we can appreciate how scientists can deduce the origins of Blackbeard's crew from the chemical composition of their bones, revealing a crew as diverse as the colonies from which they hailed.

And yet, despite the wealth of knowledge, the allure of Blackbeard remains partially shrouded in mystery. Was he a calculating entrepreneur of the seas, a bloodthirsty marauder, or something more complex? Different perspectives offer varied interpretations of his character and legacy, reminding us that history is often not a single story but a mosaic of viewpoints.

Questions linger, inviting us to ponder. How did a man who terrorized the Atlantic for a mere two years manage to become a legend whose name is still whispered with a mix of fear and awe? What new discoveries lie in wait beneath the waves or within the pages of forgotten texts? Each question leads us down a path of exploration, challenging us to understand the past and, in doing so, to understand ourselves.

In conclusion, Blackbeard's enduring mystique is

not just a product of his actions but of our relentless pursuit of understanding. It is the dance of discovery and narrative, of fact and lore, that keeps the legend alive. As we peel back the layers of history, with each unearthed artifact and deciphered document, we add to the story of a man who, in life and death, has become more than a historical figure—he has become a symbol of the wild, untamed spirit of an era long gone but never forgotten.

NOTE TO THE READER

I hope you've enjoyed learning about Blackbeard the Pirate. If you have, then please consider leaving a rating or review.

Many thanks

History Nerds

Printed in Great Britain
by Amazon

45347709R00044